The Anxious Generation

Jason Haller

Table of Contents

INTRODUCTION

Welcome to a journey of understanding, resilience, and empowerment in the digital age. "The Anxious Generation – Workbook" is a workbook designed to address the pressing challenges faced by today's youth, marked by an unprecedented mental health crisis and the pervasive influence of technology. This guide serves as a beacon for parents, educators, and adolescents themselves, illuminating a path through the complexities of growing up surrounded by screens.

Our world has undergone a digital revolution, transforming the way we connect, learn, and live. Alongside these changes, a rise in anxiety and depression among young people has sparked a crucial conversation about the impact of technology on our well-being. This workbook delves into these issues, offering insights and strategies to foster mental health in a digital landscape.

From understanding the signs of anxiety and depression to exploring the effects of social media on self-esteem and the importance of free play, each chapter builds on the last to provide a comprehensive guide for navigating this new world. With practical advice on managing technological exposure and strengthening mental health, this workbook aims to equip young people and their supporters with the tools they need to thrive.

As we explore the intersection of technology, mental health, and the developmental journey of the youth, "The Anxious Generation" encourages a balanced approach to digital life. It advocates for mindful engagement with technology, emphasizing the importance of human connections, outdoor play, and mindful practices in building resilience and happiness.

Embark on this essential exploration to empower yourself and the young people in your life to face the digital age with confidence, wisdom, and strength.

The Anxious generation

The contemporary era has witnessed a stark increase in mental health issues among adolescents, marking a significant concern that can be termed an epidemic. This rise is not merely a statistical blip but a substantial shift indicating a deeper, more pervasive problem within our society. The surge in cases of anxiety, depression, self-harm, and suicidal thoughts among young people has been well-documented, paralleling the advent and proliferation of digital technology and social media.

This phenomenon's complexity is multifaceted, rooted in a combination of societal, technological, and environmental changes that have altered the very fabric of adolescence. The omnipresence of digital devices has reshaped social interactions, with young people increasingly substituting in-person connections for online engagements. This shift has exposed them to a relentless cycle of comparison, cyberbullying, and an ever-persistent pressure to curate a perfect life online, often leading to feelings of inadequacy, isolation, and anxiety. Moreover, the decline of free play and the rise of a more structured, supervised upbringing have left little room for unstructured, exploratory experiences that are crucial for emotional and social development. The protective bubble created around children, while well-intentioned, may inadvertently hinder their ability to navigate challenges, solve problems independently, and develop resilience against mental stressors.

Environmental factors, including academic pressures, uncertain economic futures, and the global impact of events like the COVID-19 pandemic, have further compounded the mental health challenges faced by today's youth. The cumulative effect of these stressors has led to a generation grappling with mental health issues at an unprecedented scale.

Addressing this epidemic requires a multifaceted approach, encompassing increased awareness, destigmatization of mental health issues, access to effective mental health care, and a concerted effort to understand and mitigate the impact of digital technology on young minds. It also calls for a reevaluation of societal norms around parenting, education, and community support to foster environments that promote mental well-being and resilience in young people.

As we delve deeper into understanding this epidemic, it becomes imperative to not only consider the immediate impacts but also to look ahead at the long-term implications for individuals and society at large. The path forward involves collective action, informed interventions, and a commitment to nurturing a healthier, more supportive landscape for the anxious generation.

The impact of technology on our lives, particularly on the younger generation, is both profound and multifaceted, shaping not just the way we communicate, but also how we perceive ourselves and our place in the world. The digital age, characterized by the ubiquity of smartphones, social media, and the internet, has ushered in a new era of connectivity, offering unprecedented opportunities for learning, creativity, and engagement. Yet, this same technology has a darker side, contributing to a host of mental health challenges among adolescents and young adults. One of the most significant impacts of technology is on social interaction. While digital platforms can facilitate connections across distances, they often replace face-to-face interactions, leading to a decrease in meaningful personal connections. This shift can exacerbate feelings of loneliness and isolation, despite being more "connected" than ever before. Social media, in particular, has been implicated in the rise of anxiety and depression among youths, largely due to constant social comparison, cyberbullying, and the pressure to maintain an idealized online persona.

Furthermore, the constant barrage of notifications and the endless scroll of social media feeds have contributed to shortened attention spans and disrupted sleep patterns. The blue light emitted by screens interferes with the natural sleep cycle, while the never-ending stream of information keeps the brain engaged, making it difficult to unwind and rest. This lack of quality sleep can have a cascading effect on mental and physical health, contributing to stress, poor academic performance, and a decreased ability to manage emotions. The educational sphere has also felt the impact of technology, with digital tools offering new ways of learning but also presenting challenges. The ease of access to information has the potential to foster independence and critical thinking; however, it also raises concerns about digital distraction, the reliability of online sources, and the potential for academic dishonesty.

Moreover, the digital footprint left by online activities can have long-term implications for young people's futures. The permanence of online posts and the speed at which they can be shared mean that a momentary lapse in judgment can have disproportionate consequences, affecting college admissions, employment opportunities, and personal relationships.

In navigating the impact of technology, it's essential to strike a balance. Educating young people about digital literacy, including the responsible use of technology, the importance of privacy, and the skills to critically evaluate online content, is crucial. Equally important is fostering environments—both online and off—that support mental well-being, encourage real-world connections, and provide spaces for unstructured play and downtime.

As we move forward, the challenge lies in leveraging the benefits of technology while mitigating its adverse effects. This requires a collaborative effort from parents, educators, policymakers, and young people themselves to create a digital landscape that promotes health, well-being, and genuine connectivity.

The concept of free play, a type of play that is not directed by adults and allows children to engage with their environment and each other on their own terms, is increasingly recognized for its critical role in healthy childhood development. Free play offers more than just an outlet for physical energy; it is a fundamental component of learning, social development, and emotional well-being. Through free play, children learn to negotiate, resolve conflicts, and make decisions, thereby developing essential life skills such as problem-solving, creativity, and emotional regulation. These unstructured playtimes allow kids to explore their interests, which is crucial for self-discovery and intrinsic motivation. As children interact with peers in an unstructured environment, they also develop social skills, learning to cooperate, share, and understand others' perspectives. Beyond these social and cognitive benefits, free play has been linked to physical health benefits, including the development of motor skills and overall fitness. It also plays a vital role in reducing stress and anxiety in children, offering them a natural way to process their emotions and experiences. In an era where academic pressure and structured activities often dominate children's schedules, free play is a vital counterbalance that fosters a sense of freedom and joy, contributing to happier, more resilient children.

However, the opportunities for free play have been diminishing in recent decades, impacted by urbanization, safety concerns, and the rise of technology and screen time. The loss of this vital component of childhood has coincided with an increase in mental health issues among children and adolescents, underscoring the importance of advocating for and facilitating unstructured playtime.

Promoting free play requires a concerted effort from parents, educators, and policymakers to recognize its value and ensure children have the time and safe spaces to engage in this fundamental activity. Encouraging free play is not about neglecting structured learning or the benefits of technology but about providing a balanced approach to childhood development that honors the inherent need of children to explore, imagine, and play on their own terms.

To further emphasize the critical nature of free play in the development of children, it's essential to delve into its nuanced benefits and the consequences of its decline.

Psychological Resilience and Emotional Development: Free play is not just about the physical or social; it's deeply intertwined with emotional health. It provides a safe space for children to experiment with emotions, confront fears, and practice empathy. This emotional play aids in the development of resilience, allowing children to experience various outcomes in a controlled environment, helping them learn to cope with disappointment, frustration, and joy.

Fostering Creativity and Imagination: During free play, children have the liberty to invent scenarios, roles, and activities, fostering an environment rich in creativity and innovation. This unbounded exploration is crucial for cognitive development, as it encourages children to think outside the box and develop unique problem-solving skills. The imaginative play also strengthens narrative skills and abstract thinking, laying the foundation for future learning and creativity.

Impact on Attention and Learning Abilities: Research suggests that children who engage in regular, unstructured playtime exhibit better self-directed executive functioning. When children create games, negotiate rules, and decide the flow of play, they're engaging in complex decision-making and planning processes. These experiences can enhance their ability to focus, plan, and prioritize in academic settings, suggesting that free play can contribute positively to classroom learning and attention.

The Role of Adults in Facilitating Free Play: While free play is defined by its lack of adult direction, the role of adults in facilitating safe and conducive environments for such play cannot be understated. Parents, educators, and community planners can play a pivotal role by ensuring that children have access to safe outdoor spaces, time for unstructured play, and the freedom to explore their surroundings without undue interference. This might include advocating for play-friendly policies in urban planning, reducing overscheduling in children's lives, and understanding the value of time spent 'just playing.'

Addressing the Decline of Free Play: The reduction in free play opportunities due to urbanization, safety concerns, and the digital age's allure necessitates a cultural shift towards valuing and reintegrating play into children's daily lives. Communities and schools can introduce initiatives like play streets, forest schools, and adventure playgrounds, which have shown promise in various locales for encouraging active, imaginative play.

In sum, free play is a cornerstone of healthy child development, vital for physical, emotional, and cognitive growth. As society moves forward, it's crucial to safeguard and promote play, ensuring that children receive the myriad benefits it offers. By fostering environments where free play is encouraged and valued, we contribute to the development of well-rounded, resilient, and creative individuals poised to navigate the complexities of life.

Identifying the Signs

Recognizing anxiety and depression in young people is a crucial skill for parents, educators, and peers, as early detection and intervention can significantly impact outcomes. Both conditions can manifest differently in adolescents compared to adults, making it vital to understand the specific signs and behaviors to look for.

Anxiety

Anxiety in adolescents often goes beyond the typical fears and nervous moments that come with growing up. Key signs to watch for include:

Excessive Worry: This might involve constant concerns about grades, family issues, relationships, or other aspects of their lives, to the point where it interferes with daily activities.

Physical Symptoms: Anxiety can manifest physically through symptoms such as stomachaches, headaches, muscle tension, or unexplained aches and pains.

Avoidance Behavior: A tendency to avoid places, people, or activities, even ones previously enjoyed, can be a sign of anxiety. This might include skipping school, avoiding social situations, or refusing to participate in new activities.

Sleep Disturbances: Difficulty falling asleep, staying asleep, or experiencing nightmares can be linked to anxiety.

Irritability or Restlessness: Anxious adolescents may appear unusually irritable or agitated without an apparent reason.

Depression

Depression in adolescents can sometimes be dismissed as typical teen moodiness. However, certain signs suggest a deeper issue:

Persistent Sadness or Hopelessness: Feelings of deep sadness, crying spells for no apparent reason, or a pervasive sense of hopelessness.

Loss of Interest: A noticeable lack of interest or pleasure in activities they used to enjoy, including hobbies, sports, or spending time with friends.

Changes in Eating or Sleeping Habits: Significant weight loss or gain, overeating, or lack of eating, insomnia, or excessive sleeping could indicate depression.

Fatigue or Lack of Energy: Experiencing a constant feeling of fatigue or decreased energy levels, making it hard to engage in daily tasks.

Concentration Problems: Difficulty focusing, making decisions, or remembering things.

Both conditions may also present through a decline in academic performance, withdrawal from friends and family, or expressing negative self-assessments. In more severe cases, there might be mentions of self-harm, suicidal thoughts, or behaviors, which require immediate attention.

It's important to approach conversations about mental health with empathy and without judgment. Encourage open dialogue, and seek professional help if you suspect an adolescent is struggling with anxiety or depression. Early intervention can involve counseling, lifestyle changes, and sometimes medication under professional guidance, significantly improving their quality of life and ability to cope with challenges.

Monitoring behaviors in adolescents is essential for identifying potential mental health issues early. Certain behaviors, while sometimes dismissed as typical teenage angst or moodiness, can signal underlying anxiety, depression, or other mental health concerns. Here are some behaviors to monitor:

Withdrawal from Social Activities

A significant withdrawal from social interactions, including family gatherings, outings with friends, or extracurricular activities, can indicate a problem. While it's normal for teenagers to seek more privacy, a complete pullback from social life is concerning.

Changes in Academic Performance

A sudden drop in grades, loss of interest in schoolwork, or frequent absences might not just be academic issues but signs of underlying mental health problems. These changes can result from difficulties in concentration, loss of motivation, or avoidance of school due to anxiety.

Substance Use

An increase in the use of alcohol, drugs, or other substances can be a red flag. Adolescents might turn to these substances as a way to cope with anxiety, depression, or stress, not recognizing the harmful long-term effects.

Online Behavior

Pay attention to changes in online behavior. Spending excessive time on social media, engaging in risky online activities, or a sudden change in the type of content they share or interact with can be indicative of underlying issues.

Emotional Volatility

Excessive irritability, anger, or mood swings that seem disproportionate to the situation at hand can be signs of emotional distress. While hormonal changes can cause moodiness in teenagers, extreme emotional reactions warrant further attention.

Sleeping and Eating Habits

Significant changes in sleeping or eating patterns – either too much or too little – can be signs of depression or anxiety. These might include insomnia, waking up frequently during the night, overeating, or loss of appetite.

Expressions of Hopelessness or Worthlessness

Pay attention to the language they use, especially if they express feelings of hopelessness, worthlessness, or mention not having a future. These expressions can be verbal or through writing, texts, or social media posts.

Unexplained Physical Symptoms

Frequent complaints of physical symptoms without a clear medical cause, such as headaches, stomachaches, or general aches and pains, can be manifestations of anxiety or depression.

Risky Behaviors

Engaging in risky behaviors, such as reckless driving, unsafe sex, or other activities that put them in danger, can be a sign of underlying distress and a disregard for their own well-being.

It's crucial to approach these observations with care and open communication. Encouraging a dialogue where the adolescent feels safe to express their feelings and experiences is vital. If you observe these behaviors, consider reaching out to a mental health professional for guidance on how to best support the adolescent in seeking help. Early intervention can make a significant difference in their mental health journey.

Determining when to seek professional help for an adolescent showing signs of anxiety, depression, or other mental health concerns is a crucial step that can profoundly influence their path to recovery and well-being. While occasional mood swings, changes in behavior, and emotional ups and downs are part of the teenage years, certain indicators suggest the need for professional intervention:

Escalation of Symptoms

If symptoms of anxiety or depression worsen over time or begin to interfere significantly with the adolescent's daily life—including school performance, relationships, and self-care—it's a strong signal that professional help is needed. This can include a persistent feeling of sadness, withdrawal from social activities, or intense worry that doesn't subside.

Risky or Self-Harming Behaviors

Any indication of self-harm, substance abuse, or engagement in risky behaviors warrants immediate attention. These actions often signal an attempt to cope with overwhelming feelings and can have serious, long-lasting consequences if not addressed promptly.

Changes in Physical Health

Significant changes in sleeping patterns, appetite, or persistent unexplained physical complaints, such as headaches or stomachaches, are concerning signs. Mental health issues can manifest physically, and these changes can impact overall health and quality of life.

Expressions of Hopelessness or Suicidal Thoughts

Any talk of suicide, self-harm, or expressions of hopelessness should be taken very seriously. These are clear signs that an adolescent is struggling with intense emotional pain and needs immediate help. It's critical to address these signals directly and seek professional support without delay.

Inability to Perform Daily Activities

When mental health issues start to prevent the adolescent from performing daily activities, such as attending school, maintaining hygiene, or participating in family life, it's a sign that the challenges they face exceed what can be managed without professional help.

Lack of Response to Support

If an adolescent does not seem to improve despite attempts at support through family interventions, changes in routine, or school-based support, it might indicate that the issues they're facing are beyond the scope of these measures. Professional help can provide specialized interventions tailored to their needs.

Choosing to Seek Help

Deciding to seek help is a proactive step towards healing. It involves consulting with mental health professionals who can offer a comprehensive assessment and develop a tailored treatment plan. This might include therapy, medication, or a combination of approaches designed to address the adolescent's specific needs. Engaging with professionals also provides families with guidance and strategies to support the adolescent through recovery.

It's essential to approach the topic of seeking help with sensitivity and openness, ensuring that the adolescent feels supported and understood. Remember, seeking help is a sign of strength and an important step in supporting the mental and emotional health of a young person.

The Story of Technology in Young Lives

The transition from flip phones to smartphones marks a significant evolution in the way we communicate and interact with the world around us. This shift has not just changed the hardware in our pockets; it has transformed the fabric of social interaction, information consumption, and our engagement with digital spaces. Initially, mobile phones were primarily used for voice communication and, to a lesser extent, text messaging. Flip phones, with their physical keypads and limited internet capabilities, symbolized a phase where the mobile phone was still largely an accessory to everyday life, not the centerpiece.

The advent of smartphones, characterized by their touchscreens, app ecosystems, and high-speed internet connectivity, ushered in a new era of digital integration. These devices have become our primary access points to the internet, social media, and a myriad of services from banking to education, entertainment, and health. The convenience and capabilities of smartphones have made them indispensable, but this transition has also raised concerns, especially regarding mental health and social behavior, particularly among adolescents.

Smartphones enable constant connectivity, which, on the one hand, can foster a sense of belonging and community through instant access to friends and family. On the other hand, this same connectivity can blur the boundaries between work and rest, public and private life, leading to issues like social media addiction, cyberbullying, and an overall increase in anxiety and depression among users. The pressure to be always available and the comparison culture fueled by social media platforms can exacerbate feelings of inadequacy and isolation.

For young people, smartphones are not just tools but extensions of their social lives. The digital socialization that occurs through these devices is complex, offering both opportunities for engagement and challenges to mental well-being. The constant exposure to curated portrayals of others' lives can distort reality, impacting self-esteem and body image, and the immediate access to information and communication can both enrich and overwhelm developing minds.

Understanding the impact of this transition from flip phones to smartphones is crucial in addressing the mental health challenges that come with living in a digital age. It requires a balanced approach to technology use, fostering the benefits of connectivity while mitigating the risks associated with overexposure and dependence. For parents, educators, and policymakers, it's about creating environments and guidelines that encourage healthy digital habits, ensuring that the digital revolution brought about by smartphones is leveraged to support, not hinder, the well-being of users, especially the younger generation.

Social media stands at the crossroads of modern communication, serving as a platform that offers both significant opportunities and considerable dangers, especially for adolescents and young adults. The advent of platforms like Facebook, Instagram, X, and TikTok has revolutionized the way we connect, share, and learn from each other, making the world more interconnected than ever before.

On the one hand, social media provides opportunities for self-expression, identity exploration, and social connection. It allows individuals to find communities that share similar interests, beliefs, and challenges, fostering a sense of belonging and support. For many, these platforms are tools for social activism, education, and professional networking, offering spaces to raise awareness, mobilize support, and drive social change. Additionally, social media can be a source of creativity, inspiration, and learning, presenting endless information and perspectives at one's fingertips.

However, the dangers of social media are equally profound and have been the subject of increasing scrutiny. One of the primary concerns is the impact on mental health, including the risk of anxiety, depression, and low self-esteem. The culture of comparison, where individuals measure their lives against idealized representations of others, can lead to feelings of inadequacy and dissatisfaction. Cyberbullying and online harassment are other significant risks, with the anonymity and distance provided by digital platforms sometimes emboldening harmful behavior.

Moreover, the addictive nature of social media, driven by algorithms designed to keep users engaged for as long as possible, can lead to excessive screen time, disrupting sleep, physical activity, and real-life social interactions. Privacy and data security are additional concerns, with personal information being shared and sometimes exploited without users fully understanding the implications.

Navigating the landscape of social media requires a nuanced understanding of its benefits and risks. For young people, developing digital literacy skills is crucial, including understanding how to critically assess online information, manage privacy settings, and engage in respectful online communication. Parents and educators play a key role in guiding young users through the complex world of social media, including setting boundaries around screen time, discussing the importance of empathy and kindness in digital interactions, and encouraging activities and connections that occur offline.

In conclusion, while social media presents a plethora of opportunities for connection, learning, and expression, its dangers necessitate a cautious and informed approach to consumption and engagement. By fostering awareness and developing healthy digital habits, individuals can leverage the positive aspects of social media while minimizing its potential harms.

Parents play a crucial role in guiding their children's social media use to ensure a healthy, safe, and positive experience. Here are several strategies they can adopt:

Open Communication: Foster an environment where social media and its impacts can be openly discussed. Ask your children about their social media use, their favorite platforms, and what they like about them. Share your own experiences and concerns too.

Educate About the Risks: Teach children about the potential dangers of social media, including privacy risks, cyberbullying, and the impact on mental health. Highlight the importance of not sharing personal information online and the permanence of online actions.

Set Boundaries: Together with your children, establish clear rules for social media use. This can include setting limits on screen time, specifying times when social media is off-limits (such as during meals and before bedtime), and agreeing on acceptable and unacceptable behaviors online.

Model Positive Behavior: Children often mimic the behavior of their parents. Be mindful of your own social media use, the content you share, and how you engage with others online. Demonstrating healthy social media habits can set a powerful example.

Use Parental Controls and Privacy Settings: Familiarize yourself with the privacy settings and parental controls on your child's devices and social media platforms. These tools can help manage what content they can access and who can contact them.

Encourage Real-Life Interactions: Promote a healthy balance by encouraging activities that don't involve screens. Spend time together as a family, encourage your children to engage in hobbies, and facilitate in-person interactions with their friends.

Stay Informed: The digital landscape is constantly evolving. Stay informed about the latest social media trends, popular apps among teens, and emerging risks. This knowledge will help you guide your children more effectively.

Build Digital Literacy: Teach your children how to critically evaluate information they come across online. Discuss the concept of digital footprint and the long-term implications of online actions.

Monitor for Warning Signs: Be vigilant for signs that social media might be impacting your child negatively, such as changes in mood, withdrawal from social activities, or a drop in academic performance.

Seek Professional Help When Needed: If you notice signs of anxiety, depression, or other mental health issues that you suspect are related to social media use, don't hesitate to seek help from a mental health professional.

By taking these steps, parents can help their children navigate the complexities of social media in a way that protects their well-being while allowing them to reap the benefits of digital connectivity.

The pervasive influence of technology, particularly through social media and the digital world, has profound effects on self-esteem among both adolescents and adults. The digital age has ushered in an era where social validation is often quantified by likes, shares, and comments, creating a new dimension of social comparison that is immediate and ubiquitous. This digital comparison culture can lead to feelings of inadequacy, low self-worth, and heightened self-consciousness, as individuals measure their self-value against the often idealized and curated portrayals seen online. The constant exposure to images and stories of success, beauty, and perceived happiness of others can distort reality, setting unrealistic benchmarks for personal achievements and appearance.

Moreover, the digital environment offers a dual-edged sword of anonymity and visibility, where negative feedback or cyberbullying can be both more harsh and more public. Such experiences can significantly damage self-esteem, making individuals feel exposed, judged, and vulnerable. The immediate and permanent nature of digital content means that mistakes or unflattering portrayals can linger and be revisited, further impacting an individual's self-image and confidence. However, it's important to recognize that technology also holds the potential to positively impact self-esteem. Platforms that foster supportive communities, allow for self-expression, and enable connections with like-minded individuals can enhance a sense of belonging and validation. When used mindfully, technology can offer spaces for empowerment, learning, and positive social interaction that contribute to a healthier self-perception. Navigating the effects of technology on self-esteem requires a conscious effort to cultivate digital wellness. This includes setting boundaries on technology use, engaging with content and communities that uplift and support, and maintaining a critical perspective on the nature of online portrayals. Encouraging open dialogue about the impacts of digital life, fostering real-world connections, and promoting activities that build confidence and self-awareness can help mitigate the negative impacts of technology on self-esteem. In doing so, individuals can leverage the benefits of the digital age while protecting and enhancing their self-esteem.

The Loss of Free Play

Unstructured play, the spontaneous and self-directed play that children engage in, plays a critical role in the development of a child's physical, emotional, and social faculties. This form of play, free from adult-imposed rules and objectives, allows children to explore their interests, navigate social interactions, and exercise creativity and problem-solving skills.

In the landscape of modern childhood, filled with scheduled activities, digital distractions, and an emphasis on academic achievement from an early age, the value of unstructured play has become even more pronounced. Through such play, children learn to make decisions, solve problems, exert self-control, and follow their curiosity. These experiences are foundational in developing resilience, flexibility, and a sense of agency—qualities that are crucial for navigating the complexities of life.

Socially, unstructured play offers children a unique opportunity to negotiate roles, collaborate, share, and understand the perspective of others. This social interaction is integral in developing empathy, communication skills, and an understanding of social dynamics. Through the freedom and fluidity of unstructured play, children learn the nuances of friendship and group dynamics outside the structured settings of classrooms and adult-directed sports.

Creatively, the open-ended nature of unstructured play allows children's imaginations to flourish. When children create games, invent scenarios, or explore environments without a predetermined goal, they engage in creative thinking that stimulates cognitive development and fosters an innovative mindset. This form of play often involves exploring materials, ideas, and roles, which can lead to unexpected discoveries and learning experiences that structured play or learning environments may not provide.

Physically, the active exploration involved in unstructured play is vital for developing motor skills, coordination, and physical fitness. It encourages children to challenge themselves, assess risks, and push their boundaries in safe and constructive ways, contributing to their overall health and well-being.

Despite its benefits, the opportunities for unstructured play have diminished in recent decades, prompting a need for parents, educators, and communities to advocate for and facilitate environments where children can engage in this critical aspect of development. Creating spaces and times that encourage unstructured play—be it in homes, schools, or community settings—is essential for nurturing well-rounded, healthy, and resilient children.

In summary, the significance of unstructured play cannot be overstated. It is a fundamental component of childhood that enriches development across various domains, equipping children with the skills, creativity, and emotional resilience necessary for their future. Recognizing and supporting the importance of unstructured play is a crucial step in promoting the healthy development of the next generation.

The decline of outdoor play in recent years is a concerning trend with significant implications for children's physical, emotional, and social development. This shift away from nature and physical activity outdoors to more time spent indoors—often in front of screens—reflects broader societal changes, including urbanization, concerns about safety, and the rise of digital entertainment options. Outdoor play, historically a cornerstone of childhood, offers critical benefits: it encourages physical fitness, sunlight exposure for vitamin D synthesis, and the development of motor skills. It also provides unique opportunities for children to interact with their environment, fostering curiosity, creativity, and problem-solving skills. Socially, playing outside with peers teaches children how to cooperate, negotiate, resolve conflicts, and navigate social hierarchies in ways that indoor play and digital interaction cannot replicate. However, factors contributing to the decline of outdoor play are multifaceted. Urbanization has led to a reduction in accessible, safe play spaces. Many neighborhoods lack parks or playgrounds, and where they do exist, concerns over safety—both from traffic and the fear of crime—have made parents hesitant to allow their children the same freedoms they might have enjoyed in the past. Additionally, the cultural shift towards prioritizing structured activities and academic preparation from an early age has left less time for unstructured outdoor play.

The rise of digital technology also plays a significant role. Video games, social media, and online content provide engaging, easily accessible entertainment options that compete with the appeal of outdoor activities. The sedentary nature of these activities, coupled with their addictive design, means children are spending increasing amounts of time in front of screens, contributing to issues like obesity, poor posture, and diminished social skills.

The consequences of this decline are profound. Beyond the immediate impacts on physical health, including increased rates of obesity and decreased cardiovascular fitness, the lack of outdoor play affects children's mental health. Studies have linked time spent in nature with reduced symptoms of anxiety and depression, suggesting that the decrease in outdoor play might be contributing to the rise in mental health issues among young people.

To counteract this decline, initiatives such as "green schools," community gardens, and urban playground projects are being developed to reintegrate nature and outdoor play into children's lives. Efforts to ensure safe, accessible outdoor spaces for play, alongside educational campaigns highlighting the importance of outdoor activity, are vital. Encouraging a balance between screen time and outdoor play is essential for fostering healthier, happier, and more well-rounded children.

The consequences of reduced physical activity and diminished engagement in outdoor play on mental health are profound and multifaceted, affecting children's emotional well-being, stress levels, and overall mental health. The natural environment and physical activity have been shown to play crucial roles in psychological development and well-being, impacting mood, cognitive functioning, and stress reduction. Firstly, engaging in outdoor play and being in nature have been associated with reduced symptoms of anxiety and depression. Natural settings provide a unique, inherently calming environment that can help lower stress levels and improve mood. The sensory experiences offered by outdoor environments—such as the sight of greenery, the sound of water, and the feel of natural terrain underfoot—can stimulate sensory integration and promote a sense of peace and well-being.

Physical activity, a core component of outdoor play, also has significant mental health benefits. Exercise releases endorphins, chemicals in the brain that act as natural painkillers and mood elevators. Regular physical activity can combat depression and anxiety by promoting changes in the brain, including neural growth, reduced inflammation, and new activity patterns that promote feelings of calm and well-being.

Moreover, outdoor play encourages social interaction among children, which is critical for developing social skills and building self-esteem. Through play, children learn to negotiate, cooperate, and solve problems, which can enhance their sense of competence and self-worth. Peer interactions during play also offer emotional support, allowing children to express themselves and receive validation from others, further bolstering their self-esteem and reducing feelings of loneliness and isolation.

However, the decline in outdoor play and increased screen time have been linked to a rise in mental health issues among children and adolescents. The sedentary lifestyle associated with prolonged screen use can lead to physical health issues, such as obesity, which in turn can affect mental health by increasing the risk of developing depression. Additionally, excessive screen time can disrupt sleep patterns, further exacerbating mental health problems. Poor sleep quality and insufficient sleep have been linked to increased stress, irritability, and vulnerability to depression. The immersive and sometimes overwhelming world of digital media can also lead to issues of cyberbullying and social isolation. Despite the connectivity offered by social media, the lack of face-to-face interaction can make children feel more isolated, contributing to feelings of loneliness and social anxiety. Addressing the consequences of reduced outdoor play on mental health requires a multifaceted approach. Encouraging regular physical activity, fostering opportunities for children to play outdoors in natural settings, and setting healthy boundaries around screen time are critical steps in promoting children's mental well-being. Additionally, educating parents, caregivers, and educators about the importance of outdoor play and the risks associated with excessive screen time can help in creating supportive environments that prioritize the mental health of children.

Managing Technological Exposure

In navigating the digital landscape, parents have various tools at their disposal for implementing parental controls. These tools are designed to help manage and monitor children's online activities, ensuring they have a safe and age-appropriate online experience. Parental control tools can range from built-in software on devices to third-party applications and extend to network-level controls through internet service providers.

Built-in software features on most smartphones, tablets, and computers offer basic parental controls. These may include setting screen time limits, restricting access to specific apps or websites, and monitoring online activity. For example, Apple's Screen Time and Google's Family Link provide comprehensive controls for managing the amount of time spent on devices and the content accessible to children.

Third-party parental control applications offer more granular control and monitoring capabilities. These apps can track location, filter content, block inappropriate websites, manage screen time across devices, and monitor social media use. Some well-known third-party apps include Qustodio, Norton Family, and Net Nanny, each offering a range of features tailored to different parenting needs and concerns.

Network-level controls are another effective tool for parental control. Many internet service providers (ISPs) offer services that allow parents to manage the internet access of devices connected to the home network. These controls can block access to specific sites, filter content based on categories, and set times when the internet is unavailable. Additionally, routers often come with built-in parental control options, providing a convenient way to apply restrictions across all devices on the network.

It's essential for parents to communicate openly with their children about the reasons for implementing these controls, emphasizing the importance of safety and responsible online behavior. Effective use of parental control tools involves a balance between protecting children from potential online risks while allowing them the freedom to explore, learn, and interact online within safe boundaries.

By combining the use of these tools with ongoing dialogue about digital wellness, parents can foster a positive and secure online environment for their children. It's also important for parents to stay informed about the latest developments in digital safety and to adjust control settings as children grow older and their online needs change.

Balancing online and offline time is a critical aspect of maintaining a healthy digital lifestyle, especially for children and adolescents whose development can be deeply influenced by their digital experiences. The goal is to ensure that time spent online enriches lives without encroaching on essential offline activities and experiences that contribute to physical, emotional, and social well-being.

Creating a balance involves setting structured limits on screen time while also promoting engaging, enjoyable, and developmentally appropriate offline activities. This balance is not about demonizing technology, which offers valuable educational and social benefits, but about ensuring that technology use does not replace critical real-world experiences and interactions.

One effective approach is establishing clear guidelines and routines for screen use. This might involve designated "tech-free" times, such as during meals, an hour before bedtime, and during family and outdoor activities, to encourage interpersonal interaction and physical activity. Encouraging children to be involved in setting these guidelines can help them understand the value of balance and make them more likely to follow the rules.

Promoting offline activities is equally important. Encouraging hobbies that do not involve screens, such as sports, reading, arts and crafts, and spending time in nature, can provide valuable outlets for creativity, relaxation, and physical activity. These activities not only offer a break from screens but also help develop skills and interests that contribute to a well-rounded character.

Fostering social connections outside of digital platforms is crucial. While social media and online gaming can offer social experiences, they cannot fully replicate the depth of face-to-face interactions. Encouraging children to spend time with friends and family in person can help them develop empathy, emotional intelligence, and communication skills.

Regular family discussions about digital use and its impact can also reinforce the importance of balance. Sharing experiences, challenges, and successes related to digital use can provide valuable insights and strategies for managing screen time effectively. These discussions can also be an opportunity to revisit and adjust guidelines as children grow and their needs change. Ultimately, balancing online and offline time requires ongoing effort, flexibility, and communication. It's about making conscious choices to ensure that digital technologies serve as tools for enhancing life rather than detracting from the rich experiences the real world has to offer.

Initiatives for digital detox have gained momentum in recent years as a response to the growing concerns over the impact of excessive screen time and digital dependency on mental and physical health. A digital detox refers to a period during which an individual refrains from using digital devices such as smartphones, computers, and tablets, with the goal of reducing stress and improving quality of life.

Digital detox initiatives vary widely in their approach and scope, ranging from personal commitments to organized programs. On a personal level, individuals may choose to set aside specific times of the day or week where digital devices are turned off, such as during meals, before bedtime, or on weekends. This self-imposed restriction can help cultivate a healthier relationship with technology, encouraging more direct interaction with the environment and people around them.

On a broader scale, there are structured digital detox programs and retreats designed to help participants disconnect from digital technology and reconnect with the natural world and face-to-face social interactions. These programs often take place in settings that naturally discourage digital use, such as remote campsites or wellness centers without Wi-Fi. Activities might include outdoor adventures, mindfulness practices, creative workshops, and group discussions, all aimed at fostering a sense of presence, mindfulness, and community.

Educational institutions and workplaces are also recognizing the value of digital detox initiatives. Schools may implement no-phone policies or tech-free zones to encourage students to engage more fully with their learning environment and peers. Similarly, companies might encourage employees to limit email checks outside of work hours or hold meetings without laptops and smartphones to promote more engaged and productive discussions.

Public awareness campaigns and national or international events like the National Day of Unplugging further highlight the importance of taking regular breaks from digital devices. These campaigns encourage people to temporarily disconnect from technology to experience the benefits of a more balanced digital life.

For digital detox initiatives to be effective, they should not be seen as a one-time or occasional escape from technology, but as part of a broader effort to cultivate a sustainable and balanced digital lifestyle. This includes developing critical awareness of one's digital habits, actively choosing when and how to engage with digital devices, and prioritizing activities and interactions that support one's well-being and real-world connections.

Strengthening Mental Health

Mindfulness techniques for teens are essential tools for managing stress, improving emotional regulation, and enhancing overall well-being. In an era marked by constant connectivity and information overload, mindfulness offers a way for adolescents to anchor themselves in the present moment, cultivating a sense of peace and clarity.

Breathing Exercises: Simple yet powerful, focused breathing can help calm the mind and reduce anxiety. Techniques like the "4-7-8" exercise—inhaling for 4 seconds, holding the breath for 7 seconds, and exhaling for 8 seconds—can be particularly effective in managing stress.

Body Scans: This practice involves paying attention to different parts of the body, noticing any sensations, tension, or discomfort. Starting from the toes and moving upwards to the head, teens can learn to be more aware of their bodies and release tension.

Guided Imagery: In this exercise, teens are guided through imagining a peaceful and safe place, which can help distract from stressors and evoke feelings of calm. This technique can be facilitated by apps, audio recordings, or in-person guidance from a mindfulness instructor.

Mindful Walking: Turning walks into mindful exercises can be a great way for teens to connect with the present moment. Paying attention to the sensation of each step, the rhythm of breathing, and the sights and sounds around can transform a simple walk into a profound mindfulness practice.

Journaling: Encouraging teens to write down their thoughts and feelings can help them process emotions and practice mindfulness. Reflecting on daily experiences and noting moments of gratitude can shift focus from negative thoughts to a more balanced perspective.

Mindful Eating: This involves paying close attention to the experience of eating, noticing the flavors, textures, and sensations of the food. Mindful eating can promote a healthier relationship with food and prevent overeating by encouraging slower, more conscious consumption.

Meditation Apps: Numerous apps are designed to help teens explore mindfulness and meditation at their own pace. These tools often include guided meditations, breathing exercises, and educational content to support mindfulness practice.

Integrating mindfulness techniques into daily routines can help teens navigate the challenges of adolescence with greater ease and resilience. By learning to observe their thoughts and feelings without judgment, teens can develop a deeper understanding of themselves and foster a sense of inner peace. Educators and parents can support this process by providing resources, creating space for mindfulness practices, and modeling mindful behavior themselves.

Building resilience in teens is about equipping them with the psychological tools and coping mechanisms needed to navigate life's challenges and setbacks effectively. Resilience is not an innate trait but a skill that can be developed and strengthened over time through intentional practices and support systems.

One key aspect of building resilience is fostering a growth mindset, the belief that abilities and intelligence can be developed through dedication and hard work. Teens with a growth mindset are more likely to persevere through difficulties and view challenges as opportunities for learning and growth, rather than insurmountable obstacles.

Encouraging problem-solving skills is another crucial element. This involves guiding teens to identify problems, think through possible solutions, and take steps to overcome challenges. By facing small challenges and learning to navigate them successfully, teens build confidence in their ability to handle bigger issues.

Emotional regulation skills are also vital for resilience. Teaching teens to recognize, understand, and manage their emotions helps them respond to stress and adversity in healthy ways. Techniques such as mindfulness, deep breathing exercises, and cognitive restructuring can aid in emotional regulation.

Social connections play a significant role in resilience. Strong, supportive relationships with family, friends, and community members provide a safety net for teens. These connections offer emotional support, advice, and practical help in times of need. Encouraging teens to cultivate these relationships and seek support when necessary is key.

Setting realistic goals and celebrating achievements, no matter how small, can also enhance resilience. This practice helps teens see progress and builds momentum, reinforcing their belief in their own efficacy and agency.

Lastly, promoting self-care and emphasizing the importance of physical health are essential components of resilience. Regular physical activity, adequate sleep, and healthy eating habits contribute to overall well-being, making teens better equipped to deal with stress.

By focusing on these areas, parents, educators, and mentors can help teens develop the resilience needed to face life's ups and downs with confidence and perseverance. Building resilience is an ongoing process, but with the right support and strategies, teens can learn to bounce back from challenges stronger and more prepared for the future.

The power of human connections cannot be overstated, especially in the context of developing resilience, emotional well-being, and overall mental health. Human connections—relationships with family, friends, and the broader community—provide emotional support, foster a sense of belonging, and can significantly impact one's ability to navigate life's challenges.

Deep human connections offer a mirror through which individuals can see themselves more clearly, gaining insights into their own behaviors, thoughts, and emotions. These relationships provide a safe space for expressing vulnerabilities without fear of judgment, allowing for genuine self-expression and emotional release. The empathy, understanding, and validation received from others can be profoundly healing, contributing to emotional resilience and a stronger sense of self-worth.

Moreover, human connections contribute to the development of social skills, such as communication, empathy, and conflict resolution. Interacting with others, especially in face-to-face settings, challenges individuals to consider different perspectives, negotiate needs, and cooperate towards common goals. These experiences are invaluable in building a repertoire of social and emotional skills that are essential for personal and professional success.

On a neurological level, positive interactions with others can trigger the release of oxytocin, a hormone associated with bonding and trust, which helps to alleviate stress and promote feelings of happiness and contentment. The sense of security and support derived from strong social bonds can act as a buffer against stress, anxiety, and depression, highlighting the intricate link between social connections and mental health. In the digital age, maintaining meaningful human connections requires conscious effort. The convenience of digital communication can sometimes lead to superficial interactions that lack the depth and richness of face-to-face encounters. Encouraging real-world interactions, such as participating in community activities, spending quality time with family and friends, and engaging in hobbies that involve group settings, can help strengthen these essential human connections. Ultimately, the power of human connections lies in their ability to enrich lives, providing joy, support, and a sense of belonging. In fostering these connections, individuals can build a resilient and fulfilling life, underscored by a network of relationships that offer love, understanding, and mutual growth.

Educational Interventions

The role of schools in supporting mental health is increasingly recognized as pivotal to the overall development and well-being of students. Schools are not just centers for academic learning; they are also critical environments for social and emotional development, making them ideally placed to support mental health in various ways.

Firstly, schools can implement comprehensive mental health education as part of the curriculum. This education can help destigmatize mental health issues, provide students with the knowledge to recognize signs of mental distress in themselves and others, and offer strategies for managing mental health, including stress reduction techniques, coping mechanisms, and where to seek help.

Secondly, schools can foster a supportive and inclusive school climate that emphasizes respect, tolerance, and empathy among students and staff. Creating a safe, nurturing environment where students feel valued and understood can significantly impact their mental health and academic performance. Initiatives like anti-bullying campaigns, peer support programs, and inclusive policies contribute to a positive school culture.

Professional support services within schools, such as counseling and psychological services, play a crucial role. Having accessible mental health professionals who can offer early intervention, counseling, and referrals to external services is essential. These professionals can also work with teachers and staff to identify students who may be struggling and need additional support.

Teacher training is another critical aspect. Equipping teachers with the skills to recognize signs of mental health issues, provide initial support, and refer students to the appropriate services can make a significant difference in early identification and support for students facing challenges. Additionally, teachers can integrate practices that promote mental well-being, such as mindfulness and social-emotional learning activities, into their classrooms.

Collaboration with parents and the wider community is also vital. Schools can work with parents to provide information on supporting children's mental health at home and engage with local mental health services and organizations to create a network of support for students.

By integrating these approaches, schools can play a crucial role in supporting the mental health of their students, helping to build resilience, promote positive mental well-being, and provide a foundation for successful and fulfilling lives.

Digital education and online citizenship are increasingly crucial components of the modern educational landscape, integrating technology into learning while promoting responsible and ethical behavior online. Digital education encompasses a broad range of technology-based teaching and learning practices. It includes the use of digital tools and resources to facilitate and enhance learning, such as educational apps, online courses, multimedia resources, and interactive software. This approach not only supports traditional learning objectives but also prepares students for the digital world by developing their digital literacy—skills essential for navigating the internet, understanding digital content, and using technology effectively and creatively.

Online citizenship, often referred to as digital citizenship, involves teaching students to engage respectfully, critically, and responsibly in the digital environment. It covers aspects such as internet safety, privacy management, understanding digital footprints, recognizing and responding to cyberbullying, and respecting intellectual property rights. The goal is to cultivate a sense of ethical responsibility and empathy in digital interactions, ensuring students understand the impact of their online behavior on themselves and others.

Integrating digital education and online citizenship into the curriculum helps students become not only proficient in using technology but also aware of the broader social and ethical implications of their digital presence. Schools play a vital role in this educational process, providing structured opportunities for students to engage with technology in a guided, reflective manner. This can be achieved through dedicated lessons on digital literacy and online behavior, as well as by embedding digital tools and discussions about online citizenship across all subjects.

Moreover, fostering a partnership between educators, parents, and the wider community is essential to reinforce these concepts. Workshops, information sessions, and resources can support parents in understanding the digital world and how to guide their children's online behavior. Collaboration with tech companies and organizations specializing in internet safety and digital literacy can also enhance the effectiveness of digital education programs.

Digital education and online citizenship are intertwined elements of preparing students for life in a digital society. By addressing these areas comprehensively, schools can equip students with the necessary skills and ethical frameworks to navigate the digital world safely, respectfully, and effectively.

Creating positive learning environments is essential for fostering academic success, emotional well-being, and social development in students. Such environments are characterized by a supportive, inclusive, and engaging atmosphere where all students feel valued, respected, and empowered to learn.

Central to creating these environments is the establishment of strong, positive relationships between teachers and students. These relationships are built on mutual respect, trust, and open communication, laying the foundation for a safe and welcoming learning space. Teachers who show genuine interest in their students' lives, listen to their concerns, and acknowledge their achievements foster a sense of belonging and motivation among students.

Inclusivity and respect for diversity are also key components of positive learning environments. This involves recognizing and valuing the unique backgrounds, abilities, and perspectives of each student, and integrating this diversity into teaching practices and curriculum content. Such an approach not only enriches the learning experience for all students but also promotes empathy, understanding, and collaboration within the classroom.

Engagement and active participation are further enhanced in positive learning environments through dynamic and student-centered teaching methods. Incorporating a variety of instructional strategies, such as project-based learning, group discussions, and interactive technology, keeps students engaged and caters to different learning styles and interests. Giving students a voice in their learning, through choices in assignments or projects and opportunities for feedback, empowers them to take ownership of their education.

A focus on social-emotional learning (SEL) is equally important. Integrating SEL into the curriculum helps students develop crucial skills such as emotional regulation, conflict resolution, and cooperative teamwork. SEL not only supports academic achievement but also prepares students for the challenges and relationships they will navigate outside the classroom.

Physical aspects of the learning environment, including comfortable, flexible seating arrangements, adequate lighting, and access to resources, play a significant role in creating a conducive learning atmosphere. A well-organized, visually appealing classroom can stimulate learning and reflect the values of collaboration, respect, and inclusivity.

Finally, fostering a positive learning environment is a collective effort that extends beyond the classroom. Involving families and the community in educational activities and decision-making processes strengthens the support system for students and creates a cohesive, collaborative educational experience.

In essence, creating positive learning environments is about more than just academic instruction; it's about nurturing students' social, emotional, and intellectual growth in a setting that respects and celebrates their individuality while fostering a sense of community and shared purpose.

Collective Actions

Community involvement plays a crucial role in supporting and enhancing the educational experience for students. It encompasses a wide range of activities where schools and educational institutions engage with families, local businesses, organizations, and community members to create a supportive network that fosters learning and development.

When communities actively participate in education, they contribute diverse resources and perspectives that can enrich the curriculum, provide students with real-world learning opportunities, and offer additional support to meet the varied needs of students. This involvement can take many forms, including mentorship programs, where community members share their expertise and experiences with students; partnerships with local businesses and organizations that offer internships or project-based learning opportunities; and community service projects that allow students to contribute to their communities while developing important skills and values.

Moreover, community involvement helps bridge the gap between school and the wider world, making learning more relevant and meaningful to students. It encourages a sense of responsibility, belonging, and civic engagement among students, preparing them to be active and informed citizens. Additionally, engaging the community in education can provide valuable support to teachers and schools, from volunteering in classrooms to providing resources and funding for school programs.

Effective community involvement requires open communication, collaboration, and mutual respect between schools and community members. By working together, schools and communities can create a supportive and inclusive environment that not only enhances academic achievement but also addresses social and emotional needs, contributing to the holistic development of students.

Public policies and government initiatives play a pivotal role in shaping the educational landscape, particularly in the context of supporting mental health and fostering inclusive, supportive learning environments. Governments at all levels can implement a range of policies and initiatives designed to integrate mental health support into the educational system, thereby addressing the holistic needs of students.

One common approach is the development and implementation of policies that mandate mental health education within school curricula. This can include training for teachers and staff on recognizing and responding to mental health issues, as well as providing students with knowledge about mental health, coping mechanisms, and where to seek help. Such policies aim to destigmatize mental health issues and create a more supportive environment for students.

Another significant area of focus is the provision of direct mental health services in schools, such as on-site counselors or therapists, and partnerships with local mental health agencies. This ensures that students have immediate access to support and interventions, which is crucial for early identification and treatment of mental health issues.

Governments can also foster safe and inclusive school environments through anti-bullying policies, initiatives promoting diversity and inclusion, and programs designed to enhance social and emotional learning. By addressing these areas, public policies can contribute to creating educational settings that support not just academic achievement, but also the social and emotional well-being of students.

Additionally, funding and resources are key components of effective public policies. Governments can allocate funds specifically for mental health resources in schools, professional development for educators in the area of mental health, and research into effective interventions. Access to adequate resources ensures that schools are equipped to support their students effectively.

Furthermore, public policies can encourage community and parental involvement in education, recognizing that a collaborative approach is essential for addressing the comprehensive needs of students. This can include initiatives that strengthen partnerships between schools, families, and community organizations, facilitating a united effort to support student well-being.

Through these and other initiatives, public policies and government actions can profoundly impact the mental health and overall well-being of students. By prioritizing mental health in education policies, governments can ensure that schools are empowered to support their students fully, fostering environments where all students have the opportunity to thrive both academically and personally.

Tech companies have a crucial role to play in addressing the challenges associated with digital wellness, particularly in relation to the impact of technology on mental health and societal well-being. Their influence and responsibilities in the solution encompass a range of strategies and initiatives.

Firstly, tech companies can invest in designing and implementing features that promote digital wellness. This includes creating tools that allow users to monitor and manage their screen time, providing options to mute notifications, and developing algorithms that encourage positive content consumption habits rather than compulsive usage. By prioritizing user well-being in their product design, tech companies can help mitigate the potential negative effects of excessive screen time and digital dependency.

Secondly, tech companies are in a unique position to lead by example in promoting a balanced approach to technology use. They can offer educational resources and support for users, helping them understand the importance of digital wellness and how to achieve it. This might involve creating awareness campaigns, providing tips for healthy digital habits, and partnering with educational institutions to integrate digital wellness concepts into the curriculum.

Another significant area where tech companies can contribute is in enhancing the safety and inclusivity of online spaces. This involves developing robust systems and policies to combat cyberbullying, harassment, and misinformation, ensuring that digital platforms are safe and supportive environments for all users. Implementing effective moderation tools, clear reporting mechanisms, and transparent policies can help foster a more positive online culture.

Collaboration with mental health professionals and organizations is also key. By working together, tech companies and mental health experts can develop evidence-based guidelines and interventions for digital wellness. This partnership can lead to the creation of more effective tools and resources that address the specific mental health challenges associated with digital technology use.

Lastly, tech companies have the responsibility to engage in ongoing research and dialogue about the impact of their products on users' mental health. By staying informed about the latest findings and being open to feedback, tech companies can continuously improve their practices and contribute to a broader understanding of digital wellness.

The Future of Parenting in the Digital Age

In the context of fostering a supportive and enriching educational environment, navigating the landscape of challenges and opportunities is essential for educators, policymakers, and communities. This balance involves addressing the hurdles that may impede learning and well-being while leveraging the potential for innovation and growth.

Challenges in the educational sector often stem from varying fronts, including technological advancements, socio-economic disparities, and evolving educational needs. The rapid pace of digital transformation, while offering new avenues for learning, also presents issues related to digital literacy, cyberbullying, and the digital divide. Ensuring equitable access to technology and the internet remains a significant challenge, as students from underprivileged backgrounds may lack the resources needed for online learning, further exacerbating educational inequalities.

Moreover, mental health has emerged as a critical concern, with rising rates of anxiety and depression among students signaling a need for comprehensive support systems within schools. The challenge here is not only in identifying and addressing these issues but also in integrating mental health education and support into the already crowded curriculum.

Opportunities, however, abound in the face of these challenges. Technological advancements, for instance, offer unprecedented possibilities for personalized learning, enabling educators to tailor educational content to the unique needs and learning styles of each student. Digital tools can facilitate interactive learning experiences that engage students more effectively than traditional methods, promoting deeper understanding and retention of knowledge.

Additionally, the growing emphasis on holistic education—encompassing not just academic skills but also social and emotional learning—presents an opportunity to equip students with the resilience, empathy, and problem-solving abilities they need to thrive in an ever-changing world. Schools can become catalysts for fostering well-rounded individuals prepared to contribute positively to society.

Community partnerships represent another significant opportunity, bridging the gap between schools and the wider community to support student learning and well-being. Collaborations with local businesses, non-profits, and higher education institutions can enrich the educational experience, offering students real-world learning opportunities and exposure to potential career paths.

Addressing the challenges and seizing the opportunities in education requires a collaborative, multifaceted approach that involves educators, policymakers, families, and communities working together. Through innovation, commitment, and a focus on equity and well-being, the educational sector can navigate the complexities of the 21st century, transforming challenges into stepping stones for success.

Preparing for change in the educational landscape involves anticipating and adapting to the evolving needs of students, the integration of technology in learning, and the shifting societal expectations of education. This readiness for transformation is not merely about adopting new tools or methods but about fostering a culture within schools and educational systems that is flexible, forward-thinking, and resilient.

Central to preparing for change is the cultivation of a growth mindset among educators and students alike—a belief in the capacity to learn and grow in response to challenges and the ever-changing world. This mindset encourages adaptability and a willingness to experiment with new teaching strategies, technologies, and curricula that can better meet the diverse needs of students.

Professional development for educators is another crucial element. Continuous learning opportunities that allow teachers to stay abreast of the latest educational research, technological advancements, and pedagogical methods ensure that they can effectively lead their classrooms through transitions and innovations in education.

Moreover, integrating digital literacy and technological proficiency into the curriculum prepares students not just for the current digital age but for a future where technology will continue to play a significant role in all aspects of life. This includes not only teaching students how to use technology effectively but also fostering critical thinking skills that enable them to navigate digital information responsibly.

Engaging with the wider community—parents, businesses, and local organizations—can also support schools in preparing for change. These partnerships can provide resources, real-world learning opportunities, and support networks that enrich the educational experience and help schools adapt to new challenges. Finally, embedding flexibility into the structure of educational systems allows for more responsive and individualized approaches to learning. This might involve rethinking traditional schedules, grading systems, and classroom setups to create environments that are more conducive to personalized learning and the well-being of students.

Preparing for change in education requires a holistic approach that values adaptability, lifelong learning, and community engagement. By embracing these principles, schools can navigate the complexities of the 21st century and provide students with the skills and knowledge they need to succeed in an ever-changing world.

Raising resilient children in a digital world is a multifaceted challenge that calls for intentional strategies and supportive practices from parents and caregivers. In an era where digital technologies permeate every aspect of life, fostering resilience in children not only involves helping them navigate online spaces safely but also ensuring they develop the emotional and social skills necessary to thrive in both virtual and real-world contexts.

To start, establishing a healthy digital diet is crucial. This means setting boundaries around screen time and ensuring that digital interactions are balanced with offline activities that promote physical, emotional, and social development. Encouraging outdoor play, face-to-face interactions with friends and family, and engagement in hobbies and sports can help children build a strong foundation of real-world experiences and relationships.

Education about the digital world is equally important. This includes teaching children about the responsibilities and ethics of online behavior, the importance of privacy, and how to critically evaluate the content they encounter. Providing them with the tools to discern trustworthy information, recognize manipulation or cyberbullying, and understand the long-term implications of their digital footprints empowers them to make informed decisions online.

Moreover, fostering open communication is key. Creating an environment where children feel comfortable discussing their online experiences, concerns, and mistakes without fear of judgment or punishment encourages them to seek guidance and support when they encounter challenges. This dialogue also offers opportunities for parents to share insights, set expectations, and guide their children through the complexities of the digital landscape.

Developing emotional resilience is another critical aspect. This involves teaching children strategies for managing stress, frustration, and disappointment, whether they stem from online interactions or other life experiences. Techniques such as mindfulness, deep breathing, and positive self-talk can equip children with the internal resources to face adversity with confidence and poise.

Finally, leading by example is perhaps one of the most powerful strategies. Parents and caregivers who model balanced digital behavior, healthy coping mechanisms, and positive social interactions set a tangible example for children to follow. Demonstrating how to engage with technology mindfully, prioritize well-being, and maintain strong, supportive relationships lays the groundwork for children to emulate these behaviors.

In raising resilient children in a digital world, the goal is to prepare them not just to survive but to thrive. By balancing guidance with independence, providing education alongside opportunities for critical thinking, and fostering emotional and social development, parents and caregivers can nurture resilience that extends beyond the digital realm, equipping children with the skills and confidence needed to navigate an ever-evolving world.

In expanding on the topic of raising resilient children in a digital world, it's beneficial to consider the role of resilience in navigating online challenges and opportunities. Resilience not only prepares children to face the difficulties and pressures of online interactions but also equips them with the mindset to leverage digital tools for learning, creativity, and connection positively.

Encouraging a balanced perspective on technology—viewing it as a tool for growth rather than solely a source of entertainment or distraction—can help children appreciate the value of technology in enhancing their lives. Guiding them to use digital platforms for creative expression, learning new skills, and building positive relationships can reinforce the constructive aspects of technology.

Additionally, promoting digital citizenship education within schools and communities can support parents' efforts at home. When children learn about digital rights, responsibilities, and ethics in a structured environment, they're more likely to practice safe and respectful online behaviors.

Ultimately, raising resilient children in a digital world is about more than just managing screen time or blocking harmful content; it's about nurturing informed, empathetic, and self-aware individuals who can navigate the complexities of the digital age with confidence and integrity.

Resources and Support

There are several resources across these categories that have been widely recommended for supporting mental health, fostering resilience, and navigating the digital world safely and effectively.

Books

For Parents and Educators:

"The Self-Driven Child: The Science and Sense of Giving Your Kids More Control Over Their Lives" by William Stixrud and Ned Johnson offers insights into fostering autonomy and resilience.

"Screenwise: Helping Kids Thrive (and Survive) in Their Digital World" by Devorah Heitner provides guidance on mentoring digital natives to use technology wisely.

For Teens:

"Mindfulness for Teens in 10 Minutes a Day: Exercises to Feel Calm, Stay Focused & Be Your Best Self" by

Jennie Marie Battistin offers practical mindfulness exercises.

"The 7 Habits of Highly Effective Teens" by Sean Covey is a classic guide to help teens develop self-esteem and healthy habits.

Websites

Common Sense Media (commonsensemedia.org): Offers reviews and ratings for media and technology aimed at children and teens, helping parents and educators make informed decisions.

Mindful Schools (mindfulschools.org): Provides resources and training for educators to integrate mindfulness into the classroom to enhance learning and well-being.

Apps

Headspace: Offers guided meditations and mindfulness practices for all ages, including a section specifically designed for kids and teens.

MyLife Meditation: Previously known as Stop, Breathe & Think, this app offers mindfulness and meditation exercises tailored to the user's emotions.

When exploring these resources, it's essential to consider the specific needs and interests of your child or students, as well as the values and goals of your family or classroom. Always review content and privacy policies of websites and apps to ensure they align with your standards. For the most current recommendations, checking with educational institutions, mental health professionals, or technology review platforms can provide updated and tailored suggestions.

Support groups and online communities provide invaluable resources for sharing experiences, offering support, and gaining insights from others who are navigating similar challenges. These platforms can be particularly beneficial for individuals seeking connection, advice, or simply a sense of understanding that they are not alone in their experiences.

For parents, educators, and even teens themselves, engaging with support groups and online communities can offer several benefits. They can serve as a source of emotional support, where members feel seen and understood by peers. These groups often share strategies for coping with specific issues, whether it's managing screen time, dealing with cyberbullying, or supporting mental health. Moreover, many online communities are moderated by professionals who can provide expert advice and resources.

These communities come in various formats, including forums, social media groups, dedicated websites, and apps. They can be focused on broad topics like parenting or education in the digital age, or they might cater to more specific interests or challenges, such as raising children with particular needs or navigating the educational system.

Participation in support groups and online communities can also empower individuals to become advocates for their own or their children's needs. Learning from the experiences of others, individuals can gain confidence in making informed decisions, advocating for healthy digital habits, and fostering environments that support well-being.

When seeking out these groups, it's essential to look for spaces that are respectful, inclusive, and aligned with one's values. Privacy and safety are also crucial considerations, especially for groups involving minors. Many reputable organizations and platforms host moderated communities that prioritize these aspects, providing a safe and supportive environment for members to share and connect. support groups and online communities offer a wealth of resources and a sense of camaraderie that can be incredibly supportive for those looking to navigate the complexities of the digital world and its impact on well-being. Engaging with these communities can enhance one's toolkit for managing digital challenges, enriching both personal and professional aspects of life related to digital engagement and mental health.

There are several prominent figures in the fields of digital well-being, psychology, and education whose work could be beneficial for those looking to navigate the complexities of raising resilient children in a digital world. Here's a conceptual overview of the types of experts you might consider seeking out for insights:

Digital Well-being Experts: These professionals focus on the impact of digital technology on mental and physical health. They offer strategies for managing screen time, improving digital literacy, and fostering a healthy balance between online and offline activities.

Child Psychologists and Educators: Experts in child psychology and education can provide valuable insights into the developmental impacts of technology use. They often share advice on supporting children's emotional and social development in the context of modern challenges.

Parenting Experts: Specialists in parenting strategies can offer guidance on navigating the challenges of raising children in a digital age. They often discuss communication techniques, boundary setting, and fostering positive family dynamics.

Cyberbullying and Online Safety Advocates: Given the risks associated with digital technology, following experts who focus on cyberbullying prevention and online safety can provide critical information for protecting children online.

Authors and Researchers: Many authors and researchers publish extensively on topics related to children, technology, and education. Their books, articles, and studies can offer in-depth analysis and evidence-based strategies for dealing with digital challenges.

While I can't provide specific names or links to follow these experts, platforms such as LinkedIn, Twitter, and professional blogs are excellent places to start. Educational and psychological associations, as well as reputable parenting and technology websites, often feature articles by or interviews with leading figures in these fields. Additionally, attending webinars, conferences, and workshops can provide opportunities to hear directly from experts and stay updated on the latest research and strategies in these areas.

Advice for Parents

Encourage Open Communication: Create a safe space for your children to express their feelings and worries. Listen actively and validate their emotions without immediate judgment or dismissal.

Promote Healthy Digital Habits: Set boundaries around screen time and digital device usage. Encourage digital detox periods and ensure that online activities are balanced with offline experiences.

Foster Real-World Connections: Encourage your children to maintain face-to-face relationships. Social interactions outside of digital platforms can provide emotional support and reduce feelings of isolation.

Teach Mindfulness and Relaxation Techniques: Introduce your children to simple mindfulness exercises, deep breathing techniques, or yoga to help them manage stress and anxiety.

Model Resilient Behavior: Show your children how you cope with stress and anxiety in healthy ways.

Your actions can teach them effective strategies for managing their own feelings.

Limit Exposure to Stressful Content: Help your children curate their digital content to avoid excessive exposure to news or social media that may increase anxiety. Discuss the importance of critical consumption of digital content.

Encourage Physical Activity: Regular exercise can significantly reduce symptoms of anxiety. Encourage your children to engage in physical activities they enjoy.

Support Their Interests and Hobbies: Engaging in hobbies and interests can provide a sense of accomplishment and joy, acting as a natural counterbalance to anxiety.

Seek Professional Help When Necessary: Recognize when your child might need professional support. Consulting a mental health professional can provide your child with additional coping strategies.

Educate About Anxiety: Help your child understand what anxiety is and how it affects them. Knowledge can be empowering and reduce the fear surrounding their feelings.

These tips are general recommendations that align with fostering digital wellness, emotional resilience, and supportive environments for children navigating anxiety. Always tailor your approach to fit your child's individual needs and circumstances.

Conclusion

In this workbook, we've journeyed through the multifaceted landscape of raising children in a digital age, addressing the complexities of anxiety, the impact of technology, and the crucial role of supportive environments. We've explored strategies for fostering resilience, promoting digital well-being, and creating positive educational experiences. As we conclude, it's important to remember that navigating these challenges is a dynamic process, requiring adaptability, patience, and ongoing engagement.

The essence of our exploration emphasizes the balance between embracing the benefits of digital advancements and mitigating their challenges. We've seen the importance of open communication between parents and children, the value of establishing healthy digital habits, and the necessity of fostering real-world connections to support mental and emotional well-being.

"Advice for Parents" encapsulates practical strategies grounded in understanding, empathy, and informed action. From encouraging mindfulness practices to advocating for safe digital spaces and emphasizing the power of human connections, the guidance offered aims to empower parents to support their children's journey through the digital landscape with confidence and wisdom.

As we move forward, it's vital to stay informed about the evolving digital world and its implications for our children's development. Engaging with communities, educators, and experts can provide additional support and insights, enriching our understanding and approaches to parenting in the digital age.

Ultimately, the goal is to raise resilient, empathetic, and informed individuals who can navigate both the challenges and opportunities of the digital world. By fostering environments that support open dialogue, critical thinking, and emotional well-being, we can equip our children with the tools they need to thrive in an interconnected and ever-changing world.

In closing, this workbook serves as a starting point—a foundation from which parents can continue to build, learn, and adapt. The journey of parenting in the digital age is one of continuous learning and growth, filled with both challenges and joys. By approaching this journey with intention, awareness, and compassion, we can guide our children toward a future where they not only survive but thrive.